ISBN-13:
978-1523981007

ISBN-10:
1523981008

I0468299

Credit With the Joneses

Your level of income is inconsequential to achieving excellent credit. I have worked with fast food workers who could get any loan they wanted – yet had limited income. I have also worked with multi-millionaires who couldn't get a hot dog on credit. Credit is a game – just like Monopoly. If you don't learn the rules and understand how to play the game – you will lose.

–Daniel Jesse

Chapter 1

"The weather forecast for today, November 15, for Oshkosh is 38 degrees, with a chance of rain possibly turning into snow. It's time to fire up those furnaces folks!" The radio announcer spoke in a tone of voice as though he were excited for the blistering cold Wisconsin winter to hastily arrive. Looking at his watch, 35 year-old, FG&G farm equipment production line worker, Craig Jones, realized that it's nearly 5 PM. The next Oshkosh GO Transit bus leaves his stop in front of the factory in exactly 15 minutes. Quickly, he straightens his workspace, gathers his coat and his lunch bag and walks quickly through the building barely able to shout a quick, "see ya Monday" to a few of his coworkers as he focuses on getting to the bus stop on time.

Standing at the bus stop, the freezing Wisconsin rain begins to fall. "Uggggg" Craig thinks to himself, "I knew I shoulda brought my umbrella today!" Within minutes the GO Transit bus arrives and Craig flashes the driver his monthly pass with the deftness of a seasoned FBI agent flashing his credentials. Finding his seat among the other tired and now drenched fellow citizens, Craig leans back in his seat and breathes a sigh of relief softly muttering to himself "Friday. Thank God it's Friday." His mind wanders off into what possibilities the weekend has in store for him.

Almost out of habit of his now 3 year routine, Craig's tired eyes pop open just before the bus jerks to a stop at his corner on Otter Avenue near Lake Winnebago. Stepping off the bus, he notices that it has now become foggy because of his close proximity to the lake and the sudden drop in temperature.

"Just lovely" he quietly mutters to himself, "38 degrees, humid, foggy ice crystals in the air, freezing rain, and now a 200 yard walk to my drafty old house. This night can't get any worse."

Arriving at the front door of his house, Craig lets himself in and closes the door behind him. He is met with a nearly tropic like steam in the air from the pasta noodles boiling on the stove, a children's cartoon playing on the old television in the family room at a seemingly deafening volume, toys strewn about the living room floor, and the faint sound of an infant screaming in the distance.

Standing amidst all this chaos, Craig takes in a few deep breaths and calls out, "I'm home." Quickly the sound of the screaming infant becomes increasingly louder as Janet, his 32 year old wife of 8 years, comes walking into the living room with their screaming 3 month old son Kaden in her arms fresh from a diaper change. Janet briskly walks up to Craig and greets him with a kiss on the cheek,

"Hi sweetie! How was your day?" She says quickly as she attempts to calm the screaming infant and then diverts to stir the nearly overflowing pot of boiling noodles.

"Fine" Craig mutters in sheer exhaustion. "Where's Sabrina?" Craig asks inquisitively, inquiring on the whereabouts of their 6 year-old daughter.

"She is in the kids room playing until dinner is ready." Janet responds.

Shedding his cold and wet coat, Craig hangs it on the hook near the front door, then walks to the computer jammed into the furthest corner of the living room, sits down and logs on to his Ebay account to see if any of the thirty or so items he has collected from garage sales and thrift stores, then posted to the site have any bids or any activity at all. "Nothing "he sighs to himself. In frustration, he wipes the outside foggy dew from his face and asks when dinner will be ready.

"The spaghetti is almost finished. We'll eat soon!" Janet calls out from the kitchen.

Just a few minutes later Janet calls out that dinner is ready. Slowly Craig lifts himself away from the computer desk and walks over to the kitchen table where Sabrina was indicating that she was starving and couldn't wait to be served, and Janet securing Kaden into his high chair, Craig took his place at the head of the family table. As though with military precision, Janet transferred the steaming, boiling pots of spaghetti sauce and noodles onto the family table and quickly served each plate a healthy dose of noodles and spaghetti sauce.

Finally taking her seat at the opposite end of the table as Craig, Janet sits ready to dig into her plate of spaghetti as though it was her only meal of the day.

Breaking the silence of the low clanking noise of forks on plates as the family devoured their dinner, the telephone rings. Janet jumps up and answers the phone.

"Hello?" she inquires.

"May I speak to Craig Jones?" The woman on the other end stated in a rather curt voice. Janet passes the phone to Craig shrugging her shoulders and a bewildered look on her face indicating she is not familiar with the caller.

"Hello?" Craig speaks into the phone.

"Mr. Jones, I am calling on behalf of ACME Accounts. We have a medical bill here from St. George's hospital that must be paid. We are prepared to take legal action if this is not paid in the next 72 hours!" The caller emphatically explains.

"Well what kind of legal action? And who are you?" Craig inquires.

"My name is Miss. White, and I work for ACME Accounts, I have the police on standby. If you do not pay this $736.00 collection account in the next 72 hours they will be at your home to arrest you." She threatens.

Immediately Janet notices the blood run out of Craig's face as he hangs up the phone.

"…And things just got worse" Craig thought to himself.

"What just happened?" Janet inquires emphatically.

"They…they're gonna arrest me if I can't pay them $736.00 by Monday."

"Who?" Janet presses.

"ACME Accounts- I think I remember seeing something from them in the mail some time ago. It's something about one of your medical bills from when Sabrina was born." Craig explained.

Immediately the mood at the dinner table turned into extreme tension and anxiety. So much so that even Sabrina and Kaden stopped their usual dinner time chatter.

"What are we going to do Craig? There's no way we can get that kind of money by Monday, and there's no way that you can be in jail- it would destroy us" Janet implored.

"Yeah, I know." Craig agreed in a defeated tone.

Craig excused himself from the table, his appetite now ruined with extreme anxiety. Slowly he walks into the living room and stands in front of the single pain picture window. The freezing rain had now converted to big fluffy snowflakes. Craig stood there motionless as he stared blankly at the snow-covered beauty before him.

The rest of the weekend seemed to trudge-along like a blurry bad movie. Craig and Janet stayed home with the kids feeling hopeless and helpless amid the stress of their seemingly dire predicament.

Chapter 2

Monday morning arrived and Craig's alarm on his cell phone dutifully woke him at 6:30 AM. Grudgingly, Craig crawls out of bed with a deep sense of impending doom in his gut. Robotically, Craig executes his usual morning routine and finds himself at the bus stop bundled in thick winter clothing waiting in the weekend snow fall for the 7:45 GO Transit bus to be shuttled to the factory.

Throughout the first part of his day, Craig could think of nothing except the possibility of him being arrested and carted off to jail once he gets home from work unless he can scrape up the $736.00 for ACME Accounts.

During lunch, in the break room, Craig related his experience to one of his coworkers about his phone call from ACME Accounts.

Jason, a production line worker with Craig, overheard the conversation and offered his input. "Did you know that it's illegal for a collection company to make such threats?" Immediately a slight glimpse of hope washed over Craig's face.

"Are you serious?" Craig inquired.

"Absolutely!" Jason confirmed.

"You see, my wife and I had a similar call from ACME Accounts last year- scared us to death! We did an Internet search to try and find some help. We came across a credit repair firm that specializes in situations like ours. We gave them a call and we spoke for a while with a very knowledgeable credit repair specialist who informed us that not only did ACME Accounts break the law, and that there was no way we could be arrested simply for having an account in collections, they also informed us that we have a bunch of consumer protection rights and laws to back them up. There was one particular law this representative focused on during our conversation….It's the Fair Debt Collection Practices Act. The representative said ACME Accounts was in violation of that law." Hearing these words from Jason made all the difference to Craig, who was sitting up and attentive in his chair, taking in this new and hopeful information.

Turning this new information over in his mind, Craig finished his lunch and continued on with the last part of his work day with a newfound motivation and excitement based on what he had just learned.

The GO Transit bus couldn't drop him off quick enough at his stop on Otter Avenue. Craig nearly ran the 200 yards to his front door and sprang into the house, greeted his wife with a grin and a kiss.

"I just learned something that may get us out of this situation Janet!" Craig exclaimed as he dropped his coat and work bags on the sofa and immediately sat in front of the computer to confirm what he had learned with his own Internet search.

Recalling what Jason had told him in the break room, Craig typed Fair Debt Collection Practices Act into the search engine. Within seconds, there was a list of search results relating to the topic. Near the top of the list was a link to the Federal Trade Commission. He clicked on the link and the full text of the Fair Debt Collection Practices Act appeared before him.

Scanning through the 28 page document on his computer, he came across a headline which read: False or Misleading Representations. Intrigued, Craig began reading the section. Coming across point number 4 which stated: *The representation or implication that nonpayment of any debt will result in the arrest or imprisonment of any person or the seizure, garnishment, attachment, or sale of any property or wages of any person unless such action is lawful and the debt collector or creditor intends to take such action.*

"Wow! Jason was right. "Craig thought.

Craig spent the next couple hours hunched over the computer pouring through the entire document to glean any new and helpful information he may be able to use to assist in his predicament with ACME Accounts.

During his search, Craig came across a heading which read: Validation of Debts. Reading through this section, he discovered that he has the right to request that a creditor validate in writing the debt they are attempting to collect. In subsection B of this section, Craig reads: *If the consumer notifies the debt collector in writing within the thirty-day period described in subsection (a) that the debt, or any portion thereof, is disputed, or that the consumer request the name and address of the original creditor, the debt collector shall cease collection of the debt, or any disputed portion thereof, until the debt collector obtains verification of the debt or any copy of a judgment, or the name and address of the original creditor, and a copy of such verification or judgment, or name and address of the original creditor is mailed to the consumer by the debt collector.*

"That's it!" Craig exclaimed.

"What's it? What are you so excited about Craig?" Janet inquired while preparing dinner in the kitchen.

"Not only am I not going to be arrested, but I also can make them prove in writing that the debt is valid! Craig explained in a hurried tone.

"That's excellent news!" Janet concurred.

Searching through his work bag for his cell phone, Craig explained: "It says in the law that the validation request needs to be done in writing. I need to find Jason's phone number; he said he hired a company to help him with a problem just like this."

Finding his cell phone in his work bag, Craig, scrolls through the contacts list until he comes upon Jason's name and presses Call. After a few seconds of listening to Jason's ring tone, he answers "Hello?"

"Jason, hey this is Craig, from work. Remember our conversation in the break room?"

"Yes" Jason answered.

"I need the phone number for that company you hired to help fix your credit and to deal with those collection accounts" Craig asked.

After a moment of silence, Craig scribbled down a name and a toll free number. Thanking Jason for his help, Craig disconnected the call and immediately dialed the number he had written down.

Speaking to the credit repair specialist on the other end of the phone for the next 45 minutes was an exhilarating and liberating experience for Craig. His fears were calmed and his questions answered about the reality of the situation he faces with his collection account with ACME Accounts, and the general wellbeing of his credit reports. He decided he needed the help of the credit repair firm to assist him and his wife in fixing the damage on their credit reports done over the past several years due to being unemployed for several months. During their conversation, the credit repair specialist accessed both Craig and Janet's credit reports and began work on their credit repair cases.

Disconnecting the call, Craig placed his cell phone down on the computer desk, leaned back in the chair and breathed a sigh of relief.

"I think we are going to be ok Janet "Craig spoke confidently. "I really feel that this credit repair company can help us get our credit back on track and help us deal with these collection accounts."

"I sure hope so" Janet responded.

A couple hours later as Craig and Janet were enjoying a moment of calm watching a DVD movie and happily observing their two children play on the floor in front of them, the home telephone rang. Craig reached over to the end table to answer it.

"Hello?" Craig said.

"May I speak to Craig Jones?" the caller replied.

"This is Craig, how may I help you?"

"My name is Miss. White, I'm with ACME Accounts. I am calling in regards to an account that is up for collections for $736.00. It is imperative that we collect the money. Mr. Jones how would you like to make that payment today?" the caller demanded.

"I….I'm not prepared to make any payment today." Craig stammered.

"Mr. Jones, I have the police on standby. They are prepared to come to your house and arrest you if you cannot pay us today!" the caller emphatically stated.

Gathering his nerve and his inner calmness, Craig took a stand and stated "I have read the Fair Debt Collection Practices Act, and it states that it is a violation of the law if you imply that I will be arrested or imprisoned if you don't actually intend on doing so. Now Miss. White, at what time shall I expect the police officers at my home?" The phone went quiet, the call was disconnected.

"Thank you Jason. Thank you Fair Debt Collection Practices Act." Craig softly spoke as he hung up the telephone.

Janet flashed Craig a knowing look and a slight grin as she resumed playing the DVD movie.

Chapter 3

Over the next several days, life carried on as normal for the Jones family, Craig followed his daily work routine, and Janet kept to her usual stay-at-home mom routine with Kaden and Sabrina. Craig continued using the Oshkosh GO Transit bus system to go to and from work, leaving the family car with Janet to be able to shuttle the kids to school and where ever they were required to go.

On a particularly cold Tuesday in the early part of December, Craig had received an email from his credit repair company which he had hired just after the ACME Accounts incident. The email was a request for any updated information that he and his wife may have received in the mail since starting their credit repair cases. Looking back on what he recalled getting in the mail, Craig remembered getting some correspondence from a few of his creditors and some of the credit bureaus. He made a mental note that he needs to open and read the items he had gotten from these companies so that he can report what he had received to his credit repair company.

Upon arriving home from work Craig opened the mail he had received from these different companies and from the credit bureaus. He noticed that some of the companies had decided to just delete the items in question from his credit reports. When he came to the ACME Accounts piece of mail, he opened it with a slight sense of uneasiness. Upon opening and reading the letter, He noticed that the letter included new information from St. George's hospital indicating that there had been an insurance error and that, in fact, the bill had been paid through the insurance company and that no further action was necessary on Craig's part. Seeing this good news in black and white on the page gave Craig all new hope and confidence that credit repair is not only legal but completely possible. His fears and concerns were abolished.

Per the email's instructions that Craig had received earlier in the day, there were instructions on how forward copies of any of the correspondence that Craig had received from the credit bureaus or the creditors. Craig set out promptly to package up and mail the documents to the credit repair company he had hired.

Upon stuffing a large envelope of documents that had been received over the past several weeks from various credit bureaus and creditors, Craig addressed and applied proper postage to the package to be sent to the credit repair company.

With every positive action he takes in moving forward his goal of correcting his and Janet's credit reports, Craig feels more and more empowered and optimistic of the possibility that they will someday soon be deemed as "credit worthy" by the banking industry. These new feelings of hopefulness were not lost on his wife.

Sitting down to dinner with Janet and the kids, Janet commented "Craig I just want you to know that since we have been working on our credit with this company we hired to help us, I have noticed that you have changed."

"What do you mean?" Craig inquired.

"You seem to be in a much better mood lately. You come home from work and seem to have more energy; you are more attentive to me and the kids." Janet pointed out.

"I do feel so much more hopeful, It's like I can see the light at the end of the tunnel – and it's not a train this time" Craig quipped. Sharing a moment of laughter, the family enjoyed their meal together.

Later in the evening, as Janet and Craig were finishing cleaning the kitchen and putting the cleaned dishes away, Craig mentioned to Janet, "you know Janet, we should start to set some goals that we would like to accomplish together, now that our credit is in the process of being corrected."

"I think that's a great idea." Janet responded.

"Let me go get a note pad and a pen, and we'll do this now." Craig challenged.

Sitting at the kitchen table, Craig wrote at the top of the note pad: Our Goals. Over the next hour or so, they took turns imagining the possibilities of what they would like for themselves, their kids, and their family. Slowly over that brainstorming session, the list grew to include things such as:

- Stop renting and to own our own home.
- Get a second car so Craig doesn't have to take the bus to work anymore.
- Start a college fund for Sabrina and Kaden.
- Have a family savings account for unexpected expenses.

- Together, learn more about credit and what our consumer rights are, so that creditors can no longer take advantage of us.
- Find ways to give back to our community.
- Obtain a couple credit cards to help build up our credit score, and to have as an emergency financial "safety net."

"This is so great Craig!" Janet stated.

"Ok Janet, how are we going to do this? We need to create a strict budget and put it down on paper." Craig added.

Janet ripped the list of goals from the note pad and posted them on the refrigerator door among Sabrina and Kaden's artwork to be visible to the whole family. "Family goals should be visible to the whole family!" Janet chimed.

"Ok, now for the budget." Craig challenged.

Over the next hour Craig and Janet listed in detail everything they spend money on, all the household expenses, everything the kids require, all the way down to the smallest detail that they can come up with. At the end of the hour they had an extensive list of possible household expenses. That list was promptly posted next to the list of goals on the refrigerator.

"I think that what we should also do is to have a list on the kitchen counter that we can each write down each expense we make. If we can track every penny we spend, I think we will be able to find ways to cut our expenses and start to save money for the kids' college funds and for the family savings account." Janet suggested.

"Good idea." Craig agreed.

"Part of our goals is to become more educated on what our consumer rights are. How should we do that Craig?" Janet asked.

"Jason, my friend at work, is the one who told me about the Fair Debt Collection Practices Act, which is what I was looking through and learning from to help us with the ACME Accounts situation we had a while back. I think we both need to research that and any other consumer protection laws that may be able to help us." Craig suggested.

"Ok." Janet agreed.

"I have a question." Janet chimed. "Do we even know where we stand as of today? I think we need to find out what our credit scores are now so we can monitor them to determine whether we are improving or not." Janet suggested.

"Excellent idea!" Craig concurred.

After a quick Internet search, they found the MyFICO credit monitoring site. Recognizing that FICO is the score people are always referring to, they agreed to monitor their scores using this site since it seems to be the industry standard. It turns out that Janet's average FICO score was 620, and Craig's was 580. They made note of these scores as of that day so they can compare and see how their scores change over time.

Looking at the clock on the living room wall, Craig noticed that they had been feverishly planning the family finances for the past 4 hours. "Wow, its 9 o'clock already!

We need to get the kids to bed." Craig exclaimed. Turning off the television and the endless-stream of children's programming which occupied Sabrina and Kaden for the past 4 hours, the children were quickly whisked off to bed. Craig and Janet quickly followed suit and collapsed into a deep sleep.

Chapter 4

The next several weeks seemed to play out like a montage of the Jones' new life of financial responsibility. Craig, going about his daily routine, waking at 6:30 AM, is catching the GO Transit bus to and from work like clockwork, day in, day out. Making sure he asks for receipts for every one of his purchases, no matter how small it may seem. Taking those receipts to the kitchen counter log sheet to record every expense he made.

Janet's routine was very similar each day where she would make sure Craig had a lunch packed for the next day, fixed him breakfast in the morning, made sure that Sabrina made it to school on time, while she was home with just Kaden, she would ensure the home was kept clean and instead of watching the mindless daytime TV shows like she would normally do, she got on the computer and researched the Fair Debt Collection Practices Act. She scoured its pages, reading fervently, even doing Internet searches on terms she wasn't familiar with. When it came time to pick Sabrina up from school, she would pick her up, and then go to the grocery store and do the shopping for whatever they may need for dinner the next couple days. She would then promptly record her expenses on the expense sheet in the kitchen.

This pattern continued in the Jones family for many weeks. One week after dinner Janet was finishing up the dinner dishes and mentioned to Craig, "Hey Craig, did you realize that in the Fair Debt Collection Practices Act that collection companies can only call you from 8 AM until 9 PM, and that it's a violation of the law if they call before or after that time. Also, that they may call our family or friends to ask about our current phone number or address, but they cannot disclose why they are calling. I also learned that the Federal Trade Commission is the branch of government that enforces these laws and that there are penalties if the creditors violate these laws."

"Wow, you have really been reading up on this stuff." Craig said astonished.

"This is just the tip of the iceberg." Janet encouraged. "There is so much more that we need to know about our consumer rights so that creditors like ACME Accounts can never threaten us again." She said.

"Well I'm glad that we also have the credit repair company that we hired to help us in this situation. I feel that they are able and prepared to do so much more for us that we could have ever done on our own." Craig added.

"I agree. With us educating ourselves, and they working on our behalf, we are well on our way to winning at this credit game." Janet said.

"Since this is on our minds, let's take a look at our expenses to see where we may be able to possibly cut back and save some money." Craig said.

As they poured over their expense sheet, they noticed they had lots of frivolous expenses such as cafeteria expenses for Craig including: Vending machine soft drinks, vending machine snacks, going out to lunch with coworkers – even though his wife packed a lunch for him. With Janet, they found similar frivolous expenses. Things like: Manicures every other week, buying gossip magazines from the check-out line, and buying the latest novel that all the other stay-at-home moms are reading.

After reviewing their scrutiny of their shopping and spending habits, they then reviewed ways of how to reduce or eliminate these expenses. With Craig, he agreed that he would be fine with suggesting that the guys from work bring their fast food lunches back to the factory break room where he will meet them with his lunch packed from home. He also agreed that instead of buying vending machine drinks and snacks, it would be so much more cost effective if he brought store brand drinks and snacks to work at a much reduced cost than purchasing them from the vending machine. Janet also conceded that she really didn't need to pay to get a manicure every other week. She knew one of the other mothers in the area that may be interested in a work-trade agreement for manicures in trade for occasional babysitting duties. She also agreed that she really didn't need to purchase the gossip magazines. Rather, she could look at the latest celebrity news on the Internet and forgo the check-out stand magazine prices. And as far as purchasing the latest "must have" novel-Janet agreed to get a city library card which would allow her to check out the same book for free.

With the realization that they could save so much more money by thinking of alternative ways to get the same information, the same service, the same product for free or at least a seriously reduced rate, the possibilities of cost savings opened even wider for the Jones family.

Holding to their new philosophy of "cheaper, easier, and smarter," Craig and Janet went the next several weeks consciously scrutinizing everything they spent money on.

They got into the habit of asking if they knew someone who they could do a work-trade for, they thought of ways they could get the same thing for free from publicly available sources. They got to the point of not spending a dollar unless it was absolutely necessary. At the end of that month, they realized they had over $250.00 in available cash that had not been spent due to their new life-style of complete financial accountability.

The first week of February had just past and the Jones' were now firmly into their new habits of savings and scrutinizing every expense. They had been getting regular progress updates from their credit repair company informing them that negative items on their credit reports had been deleted, and that their overall credit standing has been improving slowly ever since hiring their services.

Knowing that they also still subscribed to the MyFICO credit monitoring service, Craig said, "Hey, just for kicks and giggles, let's check our FICO scores to see where we are now."

Janet and Craig pulled up the website on their computer in the living room and noticed that Janet's score is now an average of 660, and that Craig's is an average of 640. "Wow! We have had so many negative items deleted because of this credit repair company that our scores have jumped this quickly so fast!" Craig exclaimed. Janet stared at the computer monitor speechless.

Chapter 5

It was a very cold mid-February morning in Oshkosh when Janet just arriving home from dropping Sabrina off at school, noticed the US Postal Service truck driving away from their street indicating to her that their mail had been delivered. After unloading Kaden and the few groceries into the house, she checked the mail box on the side of the house. There was a letter from Experian. Recognizing that Experian is one of the three credit reporting companies that the company they hired are challenging their negative listings with, Janet opened the envelopes one addressed to her and one addressed to Craig. Reading the contents of the brief letter she read the following:

Dear Janet,

We received a suspicious request regarding your personal credit information that we have determined was not sent by you. This could be deemed as deceptive or fraudulent use of your information. We have not taken any action on this request. Any future requests made in this manner will not be processed and will not receive a response.

"This makes no sense." Janet thought to herself. "Our credit is getting better and better, our scores are going up. Why would Experian send a letter saying such things?" she wondered.

Once Janet got Kaden settled into his play area and put a children's video on to distract him, she called her credit repair company to inform them of this shocking letter she and Craig had just received.

Once Sam, one of her case managers, answered the phone, she asked him about the letter she and Craig had received from Experian.

Sam explained, "Mrs. Jones, I'm very sorry to hear that you had received such a letter from Experian, these types of letters can be very shocking and discouraging. As your credit repair specialists, we are very familiar with these types of letters. They are known as stall letters. They are an attempt by the credit reporting company to discourage you from pursuing credit repair. We do have techniques available to confront these types of issues. What we will need you and Craig to do is to mail to us a copy of your driver's license, Social Security card, and a utility bill with your name and address on it. These documents are used to verify your identity with the credit reporting agencies, and helping to keep your case moving forward with the challenge process."

"Oh, that is such a relief to hear." Janet said, breathing a sigh of relief.

Sam gave her instructions on how to mail their verifying documents to the credit repair company.

After writing this information down on a piece of paper at the kitchen table, Janet inquired, "So how are our cases coming along? Is there anything we should be doing that we are already not doing?"

Sam replied, "That's a great question Mrs. Jones; in looking over your credit reports it appears that you and Craig don't have any credit cards or any revolving lines of credit."

"Yes, that's true. Craig and I have been very reluctant about credit cards because we have seen so many of our friends and family get into financial trouble because of credit card use." Janet explained.

"I can certainly understand your reluctance Mrs. Jones. So many people misunderstand the power and importance that credit cards have on their credit scores these days. According to the FICO credit scoring model, 30 percent of your entire credit score is based on credit card usage. If you don't have any credit cards you are essentially saying 'no thank you' to 30 percent of your potential credit score." Sam explained.

"Wow! I had no idea that credit cards were that important to your credit." Janet wondered out loud.

Sam further explained, "Probably the best thing you and Craig could work on at this point in your credit repair is to get a credit card or two in each of your names. Once you get these cards open, make sure you keep the monthly balance paid down to less than 25 percent of what the available credit is on that card. If your card gets charged up to over 50 percent, it begins to have a serious negative impact on your credit scores. This is known as a high utilization ratio."

"This is great information, I am definitely learning so much by having hired you." Janet stated. "Are there some websites you would suggest we go to in looking to get some credit cards?" she asked.

Sam took a minute to list off some sites that specialize in providing credit cards to people who are trying to build up their credit.

Janet jotted down this list. "Sam, I really appreciate your understanding and the information you have given to me today, this really helps a lot." Janet stated.

After ending the call with Sam and the credit repair company, Janet powered up the computer and began researching the websites and credit card companies she just learned about.

Later in the evening, Craig returned from work. Janet was just finishing up her research of the credit card companies that Sam had directed her to. She greeted Craig at the door with a big hug and a kiss. She informed Craig that she had a great conversation with the credit repair company case manager and that she had learned so much from him. She informed Craig that they had received a stall letter from Experian, but it really was nothing to worry about. All they had to do is to send a photo copy of their driver's license, Social Security card, and a utility bill to the credit repair company, and they will be able to keep the case moving forward. Janet also informed Craig about what Sam had said about getting credit cards and how they affect their credit.

By this time, Craig had removed his coat, put his work bag down next to the sofa and had migrated to the kitchen table as he looked over the day's mail at the same time listening to Janet describe what she had learned throughout the day.

Janet also explained how Sam gave her information for different websites for various credit card companies who specialize in helping people get new credit cards to assist them in building or rebuilding their credit reports. She explained how the credit utilization ratio works and how it affects their credit score- just like how Sam had explained it to her earlier.

As Janet was completing the final touches on their lasagna dinner, she was explaining that after she had gone to Sabrina's school to bring her home for the day, she got on the computer and researched these different credit card companies' websites even further, and it looks as though she and Craig may qualify for their various credit card offers.

"Janet, I trust this credit repair company, I feel we should do as they suggest." Craig offered.

"Yeah, I agree Craig. I even have done some looking into these different companies, and they seem reputable, I feel that we should give them a shot." Janet stated.

"Ok, after dinner, we will get online and pursue some of these options." Craig offered.

After the dinner cleanup, Craig and Janet sat at the computer while Sabrina and Kaden played on the living room floor in front of the TV. Craig looked up different credit card companies and read their terms and conditions and decided to apply for their lines of credit for both him and Janet.

At the end of the night they had applied for three or four credit cards each. Craig and Janet felt confident about their decisions to apply for these credit cards, knowing that in the long run they may be earning back 30 percent of their credit scores.

Chapter 6

Within the next month, Craig and Janet had received information indicating that they had qualified for two credit cards each and that the cards will be arriving in the mail shortly. Also, they continued to get information from the credit reporting companies and their various creditors indicating that negative items were still being deleted off of their credit reports.

A week from their notice that they qualified for two credit cards each, the actual cards arrived in the mail. Upon opening the envelopes from the different banks, their hearts raced with excitement in the realization that their lives really are changing for the better. Unfolding the documents in the envelopes they cast their gaze upon the shimmering gold and platinum credit cards attached to the paper disclosures.

While reading through the disclosures, they read that one of the cards has a $300 credit limit and the other has a $500 limit.

"Wow, I never thought this day would come." Craig said to Janet.

"I know! We each have 2 brand new credit cards." Janet said.

"We need to make sure that we always keep these cards either completely paid off, or never let the balance exceed 25 percent of what's available on them." Craig suggested.

"I totally agree. We have come so far with our credit and personal finances since November that I never want to jeopardize our credit again." Janet said.

As the weeks and months progressed along, Janet and Craig stuck to their goal to keep the credit cards paid off, and to never let the balances exceed 25 percent. They continued to track every expense they made, scrutinizing each purchase to try and save the maximum amount of money possible.

Gradually winter changed to spring. Craig, having grown tired of relying on the Oshkosh GO Transit system to get to and from work, presented his discontent of always having to take the bus to work to Janet and together, they agreed that it would be ok to start looking into getting a second car.

Over the months, Craig's Ebay business had been doing well enough to allow him to save $2,000 dollars. Janet agreed that it would be ok to use $1,000 of that toward a down-payment in getting a used car for Craig's work commute. After searching the Internet and local car listing services, Craig found a car that he felt they could afford, had very low miles and was just a few years old. He and Janet went to their local bank to inquire on getting a loan for the car.

Sitting in the bankers office seemed to be nerve wracking for the Jones' as they awaited the decision about if Craig's credit had improved enough to qualify for the loan they were looking for.

James, their banker, came back into his office where the Jones' were waiting. Judging by the way James briskly entered the office and judging by the pleased expression on his face, they know he must have good news.

"Well you're approved Craig. Everything looks great." James announced.

"Really? That's amazing to hear." Craig stated in a semi-surprised tone.

Janet, sitting next to Craig, reached over and squeezed Craig's hand as they shared the good news and the excitement.

"Can you say what my credit score was?" Craig inquired.

"It was a 693." James responded.

"Back in November, my score was in the 500's." Craig informed with a tone of pride in that his score has risen so drastically in a relatively short time period.

"Wow that is amazing! How did you do it?" James inquired.

Craig summarized their financial journey over the last several months and about how they had studied the Fair Debt Collection Practices Act and hired a credit repair company to assist them in removing the negative information from their credit reports as well as to coach them on how to build up new positive credit.

"That's an amazing story- and some amazing results." James said as a congratulatory smile crossed his face.

Over the next half hour, James reviewed the terms of the car loan that Craig was about sign.

Walking out of the bank, check in hand, Craig and Janet, along with Sabrina and Kaden, loaded into the car to drive to the car lot to take delivery of Craig's new car.

After arriving at the car dealership, it seemed like it was such a quick and easy process to purchase the car. It was just a matter of 15 minutes until the keys were in Craig's hand and he was shaking the sales person's hand getting ready to drive off.

Driving home in his newly purchased car, while Janet and the kids followed him home, Craig noticed that the car still has that "new car" smell, he notices that it has been detailed and cleaned all the way down to the smallest detail. Gripping the steering wheel, and settling into the seat for the drive home, Craig was grinning with the giddy satisfaction of what a seemingly impossible task he and Janet had accomplished with managing their finances and diligently working to correct their credit. And now they were seeing the benefits and the results of what they had dreamed of so many months ago.

After parking the two cars in the drive way of their rented home on Otter Avenue, Craig and Janet stood with their arms around each other's waste on the spring grass in the front yard, Kaden sleeping in his car seat at their feet, silently admiring having accomplished such a big goal, and watching as Sabrina explored every inch of the new family car.

"I still have to pinch myself to realize that this isn't a dream, and to realize that we really have made such incredible progress over the months." Craig whispered to Janet.

"I know, and I really appreciate that you were willing to make the sacrifices along with me to realize this goal." Janet whispered back.

Standing on the front grass silently, in each other's arms for a few moments, just soaking up the warm spring air, breathing in the fresh spring smells, and remembering the experiences of the past months, Craig says softly into Janet's ear, "I hear the housing market is still a buyers' market. I think it's time we make an upgrade."

www.ingramcontent.com/pod-product-compliance
Lightning Source LLC
Chambersburg PA
CBHW070426190526
45169CB00003B/1434